Census Time in Bethlehem

A Children's Musical About the Names of Jesus

Created by **Pamela Vandewalker** and **Cherry Garasi**

lillenaskids.com

Copyright © 2011 by Lillenas Publishing Company, Box 419527, Kansas City, MO 64141. All rights reserved. Litho in U.S.A.

All scripture credits are from the *HOLY BIBLE, NEW INTERNATIONAL VERSION*®, NIV®
Copyright © 1973, 1978, 1984, 2011 by Biblica, Inc.™ Used by permission. All rights reserved worldwide.

Contents

Census Time in Bethlehem	3
Scene 1	6
Jesus, Baby Boy	8
Scene 2	11
He Is Emmanuel	12
Scene 3	15
Son of God	16
Scene 4	18
Away in a Manger (Medley) *Includes*: Away in a Manger—Precious Name—O Come, Let Us Adore Him	20
Scene 5	22
Christmas Time in Bethlehem	23
Production Notes	26
Devotionals	27

Census Time in Bethlehem

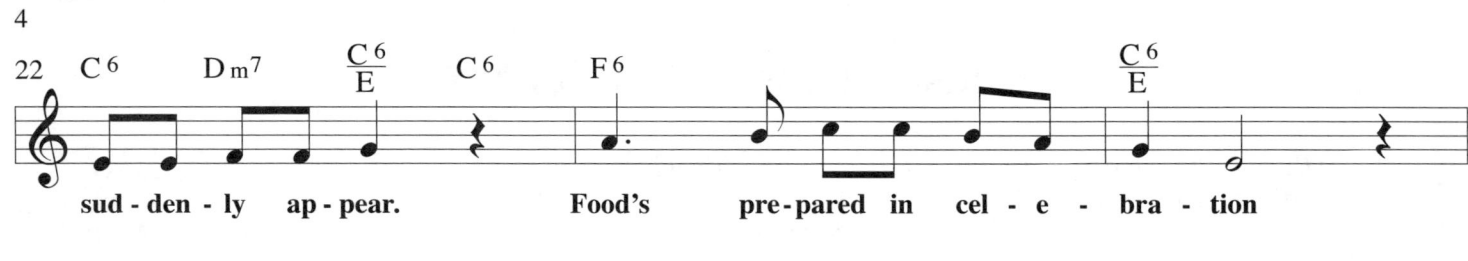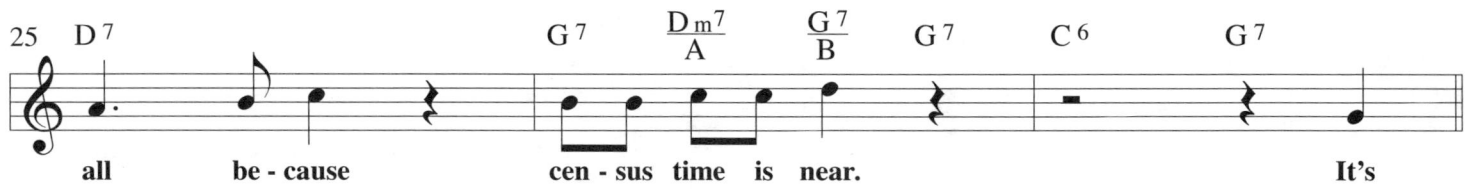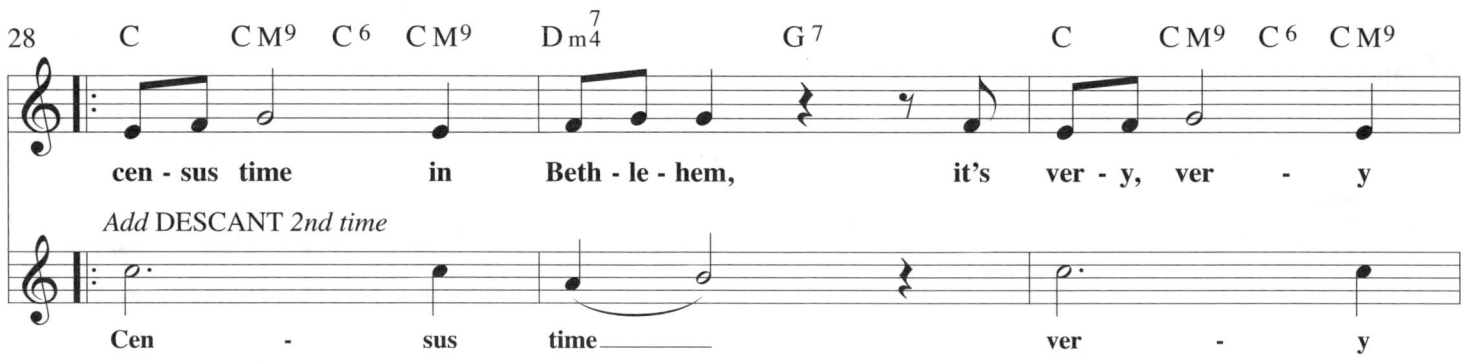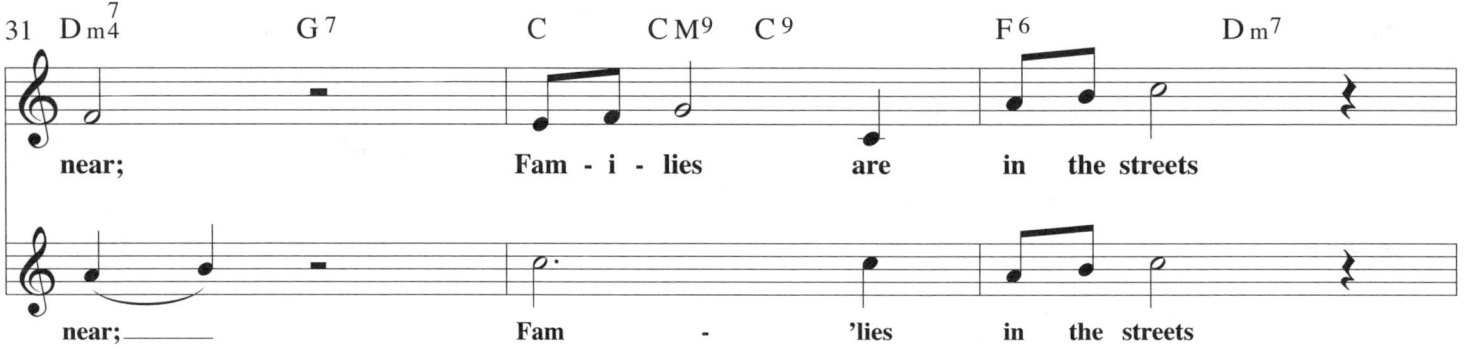

SCENE 1

(Scene up on MARY and JOSEPH in stable)

MARY: Joseph . . . I'm glad we made it to Bethlehem . . . I was getting a bit concerned! That was a long ride!

JOSEPH: I'm thankful God has provided a place to stay. It's not much, but . . .

MARY: It's not what I would have picked . . . but it's God's provision for the birth of His Son. And I think . . .

B.A. *(B.A. enters in a hurry. He is nervous and anxious for details.)*: Hello! My name is Benjamin A. Countable . . . Just call me B.A. for short.

JOSEPH: Well . . . Mr. B. A. Countable . . . how may we help you? My wife has had a long ride and we are very tired, and . . .

B. A. *(interrupting)*: The census? It's why you are here, right? Look . . . I don't have much time . . . I've got people to see and places to go and persons to count! You're lucky I found you in this stable! Of all places!

JOSEPH: Well . . . we're glad you found us.

B.A.: Good . . . good. So . . . let's see . . . you are . . . *(pointing to JOSEPH with his quill)*

JOSEPH: I'm Joseph from the line of David and this is my fiancée Mary, also from the line of David.

MARY: Yes, and we're expecting a baby.

B.A.: A baby?!? Oh no! That means I'll have to come back because there's no way you'd know if it's going to be a boy or a girl.

MARY: Well . . . actually we . . .

B.A.: That just means I'll have to come back to get an accurate count.

MARY: Well, no, you won't have to come back because we know this baby will be a boy and His name will be Jesus.

B.A.: What? How can you know? The baby hasn't been born yet!

MARY: We know because God came to us in a dream and told us.

B.A. *(laughing)*: So let me get this straight . . . you're telling me that you already know the baby is going to be a male?

JOSEPH: Yes, and His name will be Jesus.

B.A. *(laughing)*: I've never heard of this before . . . knowing if the baby is a boy or a girl before the child is even born! *(Stammering)* I don't have time . . . but I'll definitely get back to verify . . . the birth of this . . . baby boy, Jesus.

(Music begins for "Jesus, Baby Boy")

Jesus, Baby Boy

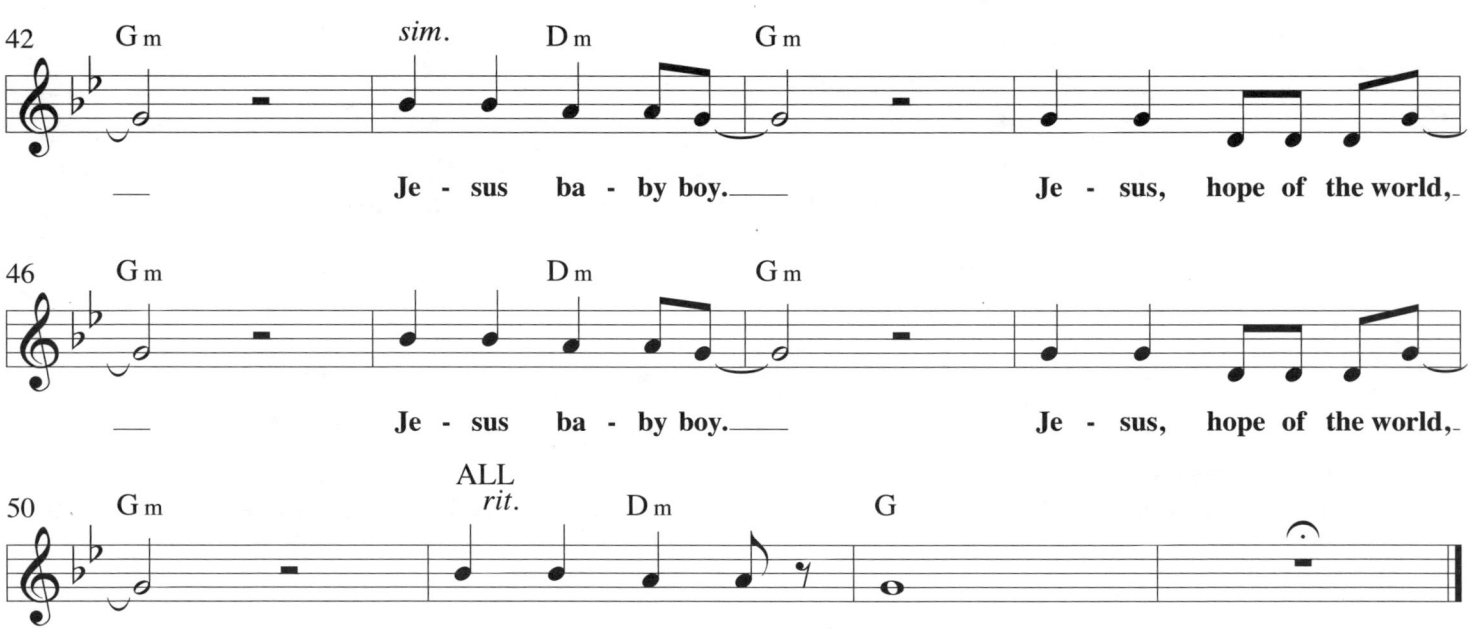

SCENE 2

(Scene up with MARY *and* JOSEPH *close to the manger, admiring baby Jesus)*

MARY: Oh Joseph . . . look at those 10 little toes . . .

JOSEPH: And 10 little fingers.

MARY: I still can't believe all of this, Joseph. *(Holding baby)* God wants us to raise His only Son.

(B.A. enters . . . out of breath and in a rush . . . nervous and anxious to complete his job)

B.A.: Hello! I'm back! *(Seeing baby)* Ah . . . I see I can now complete my census. Congratulations!

JOSEPH: Thanks!

B.A: OK . . . we'll get this over with quickly. *(Looking through papers)* Now, I've got the mother and the father both from the line of David.

JOSEPH: Yes.

B.A.: And, is the child a male or female?

MARY: Male . . . I told you it was going to be a boy.

B.A.: Sure enough, you did. Oh, and I see you said His name would be . . . Jesus.

JOSEPH: He is Jesus, but He is also named Emmanuel.

B.A.: So, this baby's name is Jesus Emmanuel?

MARY: Yes!

(Music begins for "He Is Emmanuel")

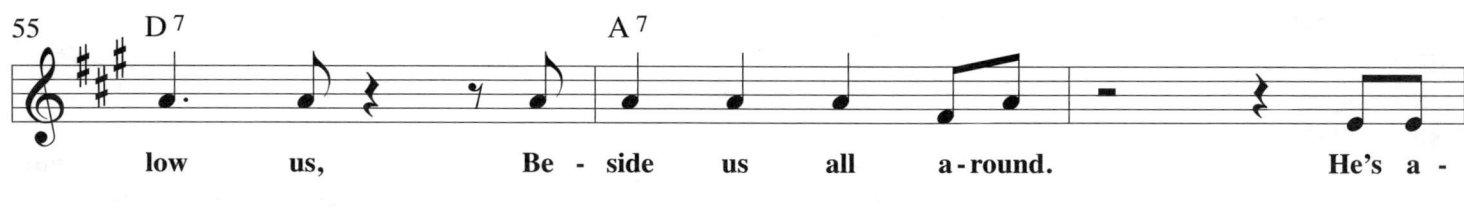

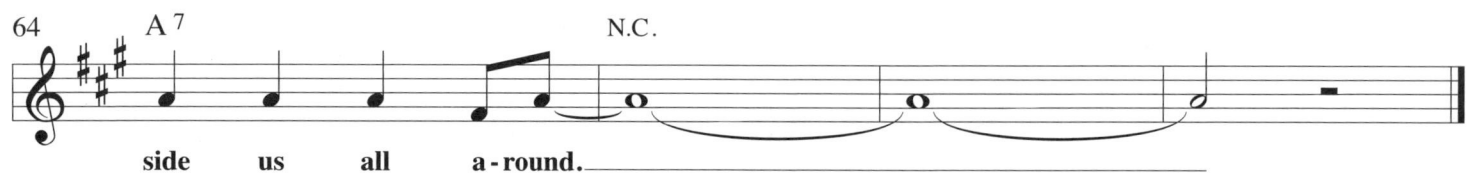

SCENE 3

(MARY, JOSEPH and B.A. are still in the stable around the manger. The SHEPHERDS arrive at the stable mid-scene.)

B.A.: OK . . . I've got it. The child's name is Jesus Emmanuel.

JOSEPH: Yes . . . but He has many other . . .

B. A. *(interrupting)*: Now . . . I've just got one more question. I need to confirm the father's full name. I'm assuming it's you . . . Joseph?

JOSEPH *(interrupting)*: Well . . . actually. The Father is God.

B.A.: What?

JOSEPH: This baby is the Son of God.

MARY: Yes . . . He's amazing!

B.A.: What are you saying?

SHEPHERD 1 *(looking in; interrupting and calling to others)*: Hurry . . . this is the place. We've found him.

(The SHEPHERDS crowd into the manger scene and look at the manger.)

SHEPHERD 2: Look . . . just like the angel said . . . the baby is lying in cloths in a manger!

SHEPHERD 3 *(in awe)*: Wow! Beautiful! Unbelievable!

MARY / JOSEPH / SHEPHERDS: Amazing!

(Music begins for "Son of God." B.A. looks through his papers and at the child during the entire song, acting very confused and perplexed)

Son of God

with
Angels We Have Heard on High

Words and Music by
CHERRY GARASI,
PAMELA VANDEWALKER
and Traditional French Carol

© 2011 by PsalmSinger Music/BMI (admin. by Music Services). All rights reserved.

PLEASE NOTE: Copying of this product is NOT covered by CCLI licenses. For CCLI information call 1-800-234-2446.

SCENE 4

(All still at the manger/stable. SHEPHERDS *turn toward audience and address lines.)*

B.A.: OK . . . I can see this baby is amazing . . . so, for now, I'm going to leave the father's name blank. But I've got to ask you shepherds . . . are you registered for the census?

SHEPHERD 3: Who are you?

B.A.: Well I'm B. A. Countable, official Roman Census worker. If you don't mind . . . I've got a job to do . . . and this one baby is proving to be quite unprecedented. How did you know about this birth?

SHEPHERD 1: Well . . . we were out in the fields watching the sheep and an angel of the Lord came and the glory of the Lord was in the sky.

SHEPHERD 2: It really scared us!

SHEPHERD 3: But the angel said, "Do not be afraid. I bring you good news that will cause great joy for all the people. Today in the town of David a Savior has been born to you; He is the Messiah, the Lord."

SHEPHERD 1: Then the angel told us that we would find the baby right here in Bethlehem. So then . . . *(excitement building)*

SHEPHERD 2: All of a sudden a bunch of angels started praising God and saying, "Glory to God in the highest heaven, and on earth peace to those on whom His favor rests."

SHEPHERD 3: So after all the angels left we said, "Let's go to Bethlehem and see this thing that has happened, which the Lord told us about." We are so honored to be here.

MARY: We're happy to have you.

B.A.: Excuse me . . . let me ask you . . . are you undocumented workers? Or have you registered in your own town? I need to get an accurate count.

SHEPHERD 1: We have already registered. But we had to come and see the Messiah . . . the Savior.

B.A.: OK . . . now are you referring to one male child I have registered as Jesus Emmanuel.

JOSEPH: Well . . . He's more than just Jesus Emmanuel.

SHEPHERD 1: He is Wonderful Counselor!

SHEPHERD 2: Mighty God!

SHEPHERD 3: Everlasting Father!

JOSEPH: Prince of Peace. *(Pause)* B.A., can't you see . . . this Child is the long awaited One . . . the One prophesied. He is worthy to be loved and adored. God has chosen all of us to witness this miracle.

(Music begins for "Away in a Manger (Medley)." Note: At the end of the song an invitation or brief plan of salvation could be offered here to audience by pastor or staff, or director. Then, move into closing scene and closer song.)

Away in a Manger (Medley)

with
Precious Name
O Come, Let Us Adore Him

Anonymous

JAMES MURRAY and
PAMELA VANDEWALKER

CD: 5
CD: 11

Gently ♩ = ca. 124

A - way in a man - ger, no crib for a bed, The lit - tle Lord Je - sus laid down His sweet head. The stars in the sky look down where He lay, The lit - tle Lord Je - sus a - sleep on the hay. Pre - cious

*"Precious Name"

name, O how sweet; Hope of earth and

---

*Words by LYDIA BAXTER; Music by WILLIAM H. DOANE. Arr. © 2011 by PsalmSinger Music/BMI (admin. by Music Services). All rights reserved.
© 2011 by PsalmSinger Music/BMI (admin. by Music Services). All rights reserved.

PLEASE NOTE: Copying of this product is NOT covered by CCLI licenses. For CCLI information call 1-800-234-2446.

SCENE 5

(B.A., MARY and JOSEPH step out of the cave/stable and stand facing audience, talking to one another, but toward the audience)

B.A.: I think I do understand, now. I'm slowly getting it. *(Putting down papers)* This Child is the Messiah, the Son of the Living God, Jesus the Christ.

MARY: Yes! This is the long-awaited King.

JOSEPH: B.A., we celebrate Christ this day!

(Music begins for "Christmas Time in Bethlehem")

Christmas Time in Bethlehem

© 2011 by PsalmSinger Music/BMI (admin. by Music Services). All rights reserved.

PLEASE NOTE: Copying of this product is NOT covered by CCLI licenses. For CCLI information call 1-800-234-2446.

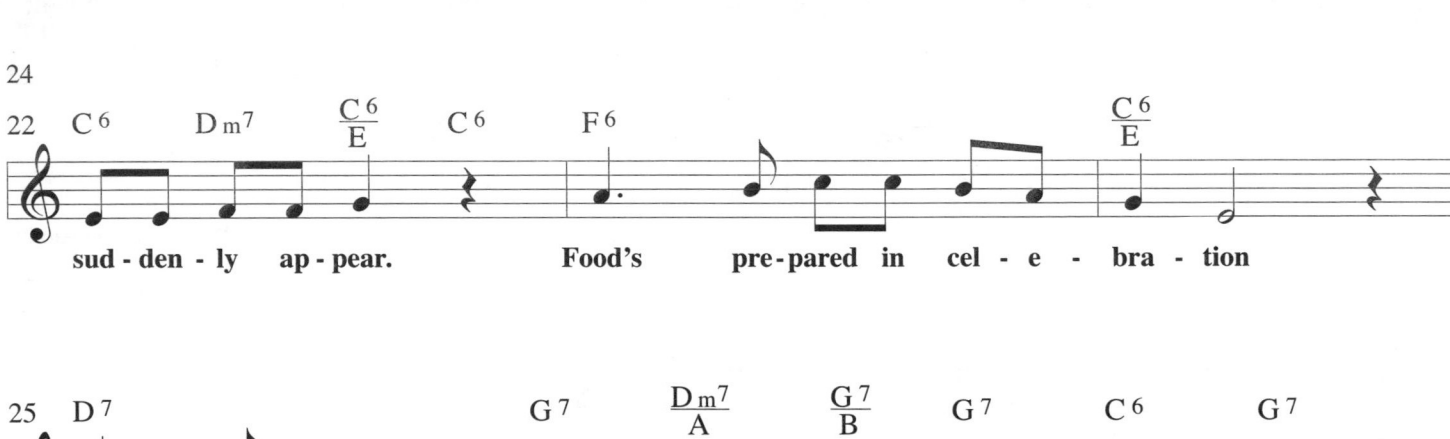
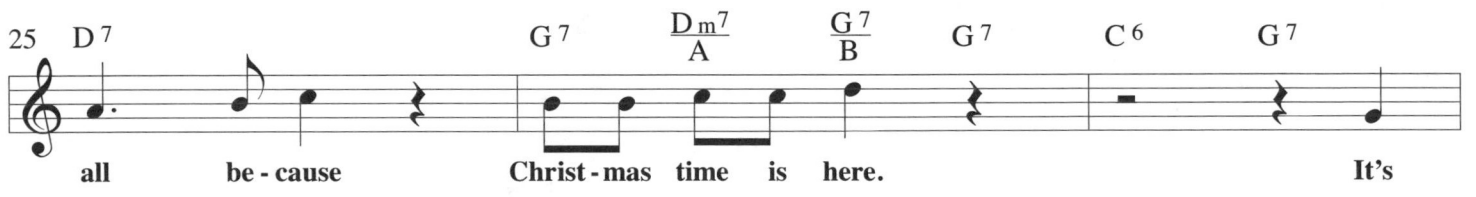

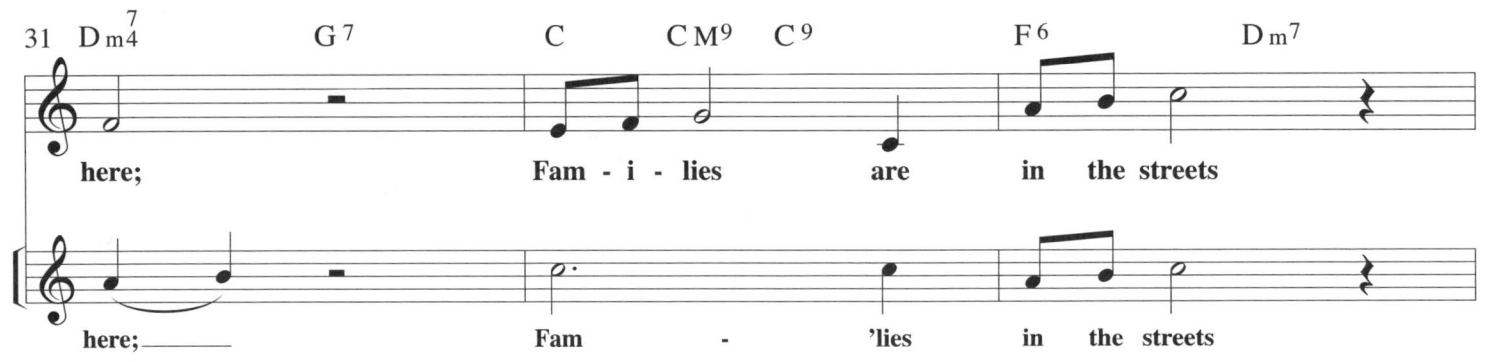
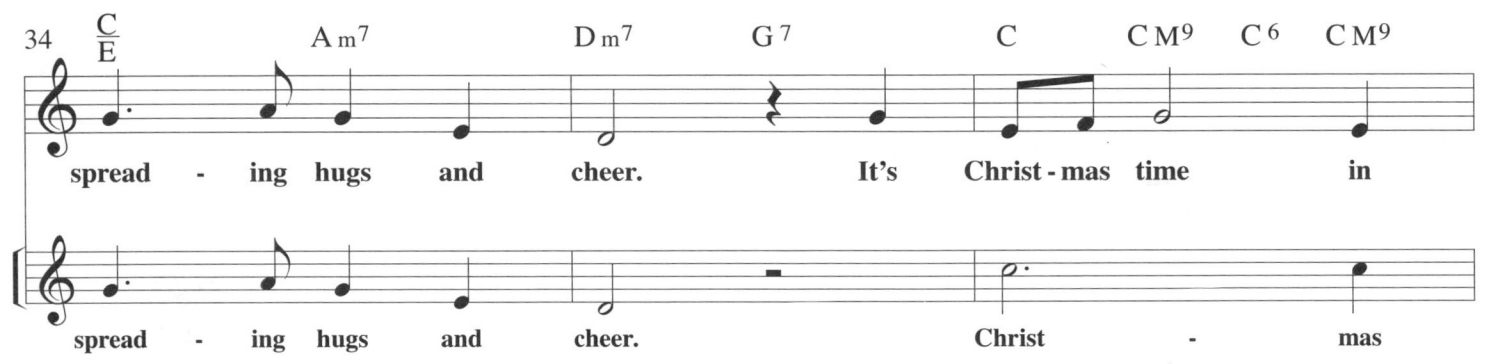

Production Notes

CAST

MARY	Mother of Jesus (Girl)
JOSEPH	Earthly Father of Jesus (Boy)
B.A. COUNTABLE	Census Taker (Boy - funny, nervous)
SHEPHERD #1	Shepherd (Boy or Girl)
SHEPHERD #2	Shepherd (Boy or Girl)
SHEPHERD #3	Shepherd (Boy or Girl)
STREET SCENE PERSONS	Optional (Boys and Girls)

PROPS

Stable / Cave setting with manger - Straw, bails of hay, cut outs of animals

Bethlehem Street Scene items - baskets, bird cages, jugs, bowls, blankets, sticks tied together, flowers, bread, fruit

Biblical Costumes - for Shepherds

Staff or Walking Stick - for Shepherds

Note: All sets and props can be as simple or elaborate as you would like to fit your performance situation.

STAGING

Set the Nativity/ Manger Setting to one side of stage. Choir in center stage or to other side, on risers or standing in rows on floor of stage.

*Select few Street Scene kids and have them mingle in the front of the stage carrying props listed above, in the opening and closing songs: "Census Time in Bethlehem" and "Christmas Time in Bethlehem."

Shepherds may enter from any side of stage and arrive at the manger.

CENSUS TIME IN BETHLEHEM

Advent Devotionals

Week One

Watching and Waiting . . .

Emmanuel means "God with us!" That name is an exciting name of God. God is with you – He is ready to hear your prayer; He is able to help you through challenges and difficulties. God is with you every moment of the day. If you talk to God and depend on Him, you can be certain He is there ready to hear, help and love you.

This name of God means God is with you personally but, it also means God is with the whole world. God is directing events in the world and caring for all people in every nation. Remember Emmanuel came to save the WORLD from their sins.

Watching and waiting . . . As we wait for the coming of the celebration of Emmanuel:

If God is with you, what are you doing to share Christ with your world or family, friends and neighbors? Right now, ask God to help you know what you can do to tell others about Emmanuel. As God speaks to you, act on His nudge; share with everyone about Jesus' birth just like Isaiah did when He wrote Isaiah 7:14!

CENSUS TIME IN BETHLEHEM

Advent Devotionals

Week Two

Watching and Waiting . . .

Jesus is God's Son. Jesus is fully human and completely God. That idea is too big for us to understand. You must accept that Jesus is God's Son by faith. Instead of spending time in doubt or trying to understand that truth, follow the example of the wise men.

Matthew 2:10-11 says, "When they saw the star, they were overjoyed. On coming to the house, they saw the child with his mother Mary, and they bowed down and worshiped him. The wise men bowed and worshiped the baby Jesus – they focused completely on Christ and told Him how great He is. They had joy and shared that joy with others.

Watching and waiting . . . As we wait for the coming of the celebration of Jesus, God's Son:

Do you have joy in your life? Have you worshiped God today? Stop and worship Jesus – God's only Son.

CENSUS TIME IN BETHLEHEM

Advent Devotionals

Week Three

Watching and Waiting . . .

Whenever someone is expecting a baby it is an exciting time. Parents prepare for the birth by creating a special room, getting furniture, supplies and clothes. They spend time thinking of a name and they announce to everyone they are having a baby!

God was no different with His Son, Jesus. He prepared for His amazing Boy by announcing His birth hundreds of years before He was born. Prophets foretold the birth of this amazing Child. Check it out by looking up Isaiah 7:14 in the Bible. God spent time naming His child. Now read Isaiah 9:6-7. Can you name some names given to this amazing Child? Jesus has a lot of names because He is so special.

When baby Jesus was born, God sent another birth announcement; the shepherds were the first to hear about it from the angels! Read about that announcement in Luke 2:8-14.

Finally, God prepared a remarkable place for His Son to be born. Jesus was born in a stable in Bethlehem.

Watching and waiting . . . As we wait for the coming of the celebration of Jesus, God's Son:

What is your favorite name for God's Son? We can still announce the birth of Jesus; what can you do today to announce this birth that changed the world?

CENSUS TIME IN BETHLEHEM

Advent Devotionals

Week Four

Watching and Waiting . . .

The wise men knew Jesus was the King of the Jews (see Matthew 2:2). They recognized that He is King of all kings and Lord of all lords. Jesus is the best, greatest, strongest, highest and most loving King ever! Because they knew how amazing and wonderful Jesus is, they gave Him their best. Matthew 2:11 says, " . . . they opened their treasures and presented Him with gifts of gold, frankincense and myrrh."

The wise men gave Him their best gifts.

Watching and waiting . . . As we wait for the coming of the celebration of Emmanuel:

Is Jesus worth your best? Jesus deserves your best in your actions and your speech. Do something great for Jesus by giving Him your best because He is King of kings!

CENSUS TIME IN BETHLEHEM

Advent Devotionals

Week Five

Watching and Waiting . . .

I have two brothers. My oldest brother Phil liked to relentlessly tease me. I would run to my other brother, Van, and ask him to save me from the torment of Phil. Van always came through and rescued me from the fun-loving taunts of my oldest brother. Van rescued or delivered me from something; he saved me.

I have a much bigger rescuer in my life than my brother (although my brother is great); I have a Savior – Jesus. The name Jesus means "the Lord saves." Jesus was sent to this earth to be a Savior (see Luke 2:11). He can save each person from their sins for all eternity (read Matthew 1:20-21), if they believe in Him.

Watching and waiting . . . As we wait for the coming of the celebration of Emmanuel:

Do you know Jesus as your Savior? This Christmas season would be a wonderful time to connect with Jesus. Ask your mom, dad, or teacher to tell you more about the Savior, Christ the Lord.